Gioachino ROSSINI

INTRODUCTION, THEME AND VARIATIONS FOR CLARINET

Edited by Charles Neidich

Piano

LAUREN KEISER
MUSIC PUBLISHING

Rossini, Introduction, Theme and Variations

Very little is known about the genesis of the Introduction, Theme and Variations. In fact, there is no evidence that Rossini actually wrote the work. It is not listed in any scholarly catalogues of Rossini's works. An old set of Breitkopf & Härtel parts exists as well as a florid and very awkwardly ornamented manuscript clarinet part definitely not in Rossini's hand. As far as I know, there is nothing else. Nevertheless, it remains one of the most popular virtuosic works for clarinet and piano or small orchestra and one of the most challenging works for clarinet of the early 19th century.

The arias on which the work is based, however, are not only definitely by Rossini, they are two of his most beautiful arias coming from two of the eight dramatic operas (opera seria) he wrote while he was Director of Music in Naples. Rossini may be more famous for his comic operas, but comedy was only one side of his genius. In his day, his dramatic side was, if anything, more prevalent and the two operas in question are two of his most striking dramatic works: *Mosè in Egite* (Moses in Egypt) which he wrote in 1818 after Francesco Ringhieri's play, L'Osiride, taken from the story of the Exodus of the Israelites from Egypt and *La Donna de Lago* (The Lady of the Lake) which he wrote in 1819 based on the poem of the same title by Sir Walter Scott.

It is important for the performer of the Introduction, Theme and Variations to understand that when it was composed, both the performers and the audience knew the arias and the operas very well. In an age before recorded performance, arrangements were the way people were able to listen to their favorite musical works and popular tunes with florid variations were the ideal way virtuosi could both move and impress those who came to listen to them. The point of the performance was not only to dazzle; it was to present a version of the famous melody which would remind the listeners of the emotional impact of the original. Nowadays, too often performers approach works such as the one in this edition as technical exercises with little sense of any connection with the source of the arrangement.

This is not the place to give a detailed synopsis of these works, but a brief explanation of the drama surrounding the two arias should help foster a basic understanding of the character one should try to communicate. Hopefully, it will also peak enough interest for whoever is performing these variations to listen to the operas and to appreciate their inventiveness, their beauty and their drama.

Mosè in Egite

Mosè in Egite, one of Rossini's most original operas combines the story of the Exodus from Egypt with a romantic subplot involving Osiride, the son of the Pharaoh, who is in love with Elcia, a young Jewish girl. The aria, *La pace mia smarrita* (My peace is lost, Ah, I breathe! I hope my wishes will be seconded in Heaven) on which the introduction is based is from the beginning of the 2nd act sung by Amaltea, Pharoah's wife, who is sympathetic to the plight of the Israelites, after Moses enlists her help to make sure the Pharoah does not go back again on his word to let the Israelites leave. The text of the aria is as follows:

La pace mia smarrita	*My peace is lost*
Ah! respirar vorrei!	*Ah! I breathe*
Spero che i voti miei	*I hope that my wishes*
Il Ciel seconderà.	*Will be seconded in Heaven*

La Donna del Lago

La Donna del Lago, set in then exotic Scotland, combines political rebellion and a love triangle. The leader of the Scottish highlanders, Rodrigo (Roderick Dhu in Scott's poem) together with his closest friends, Malcolm Graeme and Douglas of Angus plot to overthrow Giacomo (King James V of Scotland). Douglas has promised his daughter Elena (Ellen in the poem) to Rodrigo, however Elena and Malcolm have secretly been in love.

Malcolm arrives, unbeknownst to Elena, and overhears Douglas telling her of his plans for her marriage to Rodrigo thus bringing us to the wonderful aria, *Mura felice ... Elena! oh tu, che chiamo ... Oh quante lacrime finor versai.* Malcolm, the part sung by a contralto, first sees her, remembers their lovely times together and notices that she does not look as happy and carefree as before. He overhears Douglas' plans for Elena, is distraught, but even so declares his eternal love for her. After Douglas leaves, he makes himself known to Elena and in a subsequent duet they reaffirm their love for each-other.

The theme of the variations is taken from the final part of the aria where Malcolm, though distraught, affirms his love for Elena.

Here is the text: (trans. Robert Levine)

Oh quante lacrime finor versai   *Oh how many tears I've shed,*

lungi languendo da' tuoi bei rai!   *languishing far from your lovely eyes*

ogn'altro oggetto è a me funesto;   *Everything else is dreary to me;*

tutto è imperfetto, tutto detesto;   *all is imperfect, I detest it all;*

di luce il cielo no, più non brilla,   *the sky no longer shines with light,*

più non sfavilla astro per me.   *the stars no longer gleam for me.*

Cara! Tu sola mi dai la calma,   *Darling! you alone give me peace,*

tu rendi all'alma grata mercé!   *and I render you my grateful thanks!*

The question still remains, did Rossini compose the Introduction, Theme and Variations? I would say, however, that in the end the authorship is not so important. It is a brilliant work which combines affect and virtuosity in a way worthy of the best operatic arrangements of the 19th century. Rossini may very well have written it. Naples was home to many virtuoso clarinetists, the most famous of whom, Ferdinando Sebastiani, a younger contemporary of Rossini who was himself an accomplished composer and who, for sure, knew the Rossini operas very well, may also be a prime candidate for the composer of the work. Whoever wrote it, there are moments, for instance the **Largo Minore,** of the type of genius worthy of Rossini.

I have tried not to clutter the score with markings, however, as the original material is virtually devoid of markings, I have put in phrase marks and articulations which, I hope, will help convey the sense of "bel canto" flexibility so important to Rossini. These, of course, are only my suggestions. Please feel free to use your own creativity to make the edition your own. For fun, I have also included a few colorful Italian musical terms which would have been typical had the work been published in Italy in the early 19th century. Finally, I have included notes explaining certain textual corrections I have made as well as explanations for the execution of certain phrases which I have often heard performed in a way ignorant of bel canto tradition. I have also included my favorite fingerings for some of the more difficult passages.

Enjoy,

Charles Neidich

Translations

a piacere as you wish, freely

a tempo resume tempo

con with

con affezione with warmth, tenderness, affection

grazioso gracefully, elegantly

maestoso majestic, dignified

ossia alternate version

più more

più mosso more motion, faster

poco a little

rallentando (rall.) gradually slowing down

risolutamente   boldy, resolutely

risoluto bold, resolute

ritenuto held back, suddenly slower

senza   without

senza affretare without rushing

singhiozzando   sobbing, crying

INTRODUCTION, THEME and VARIATIONS
for Clarinet in B♭ and Piano

Edited with a Newly Arranged
Piano Part by Charles Neidich

GIOACCHINO ROSSINI
(1792–1868)

6

10

Gioachino ROSSINI

INTRODUCTION, THEME AND VARIATIONS FOR CLARINET

Edited by Charles Neidich

Clarinet in Bb

LAUREN KEISER
MUSIC PUBLISHING

2

Notes

1) m. 11

The G should be played before the beat.
It is not an appoggiatura, but rather
an instrumental indication of what would
have been a graceful vocal portamento.

2) m. 16

Trill from the upper note,
leaning on the initial A.

3) m. 18

It is important to play ornaments such as
the turn above as a definite rhythmic
subdivision of the larger beat. They should
be elegant and well formed.

4) m. 21. Two possibilities for playing the appoggiatura F (there are more).

This is not a good possibility. The initial appoggiatura F should resolve
to the final E. In this version it first resolves after the first F and then again.
When the F is too short, it sounds as if it resolves once too early and then again.

5) m. 39. Suggested fingerings (F and A)

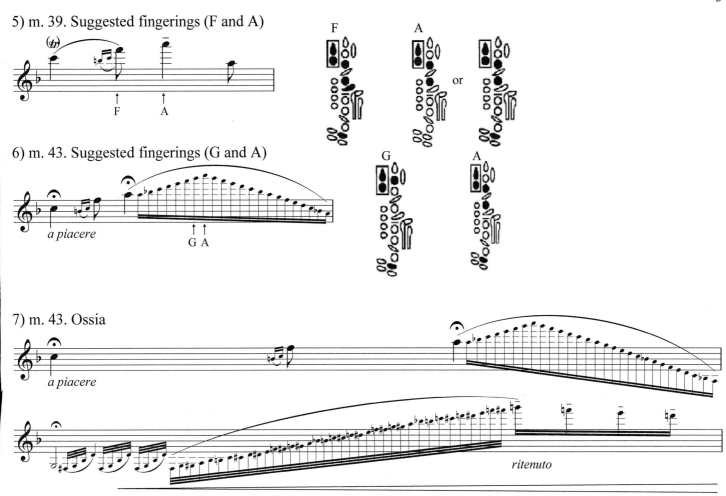

6) m. 43. Suggested fingerings (G and A)

7) m. 43. Ossia

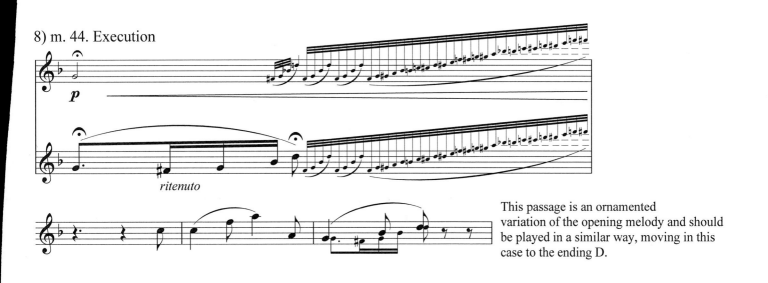

8) m. 44. Execution

This passage is an ornamented variation of the opening melody and should be played in a similar way, moving in this case to the ending D.

9) m. 44. Suggested fingerings (G)

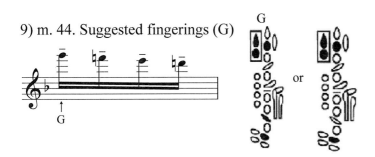

4

10) mm. 53–60. Rossini's original melody. The top line is the orchestral prelude; the lower line is the beginning of the aria.

oh quan te   la - gri me   fi - nor ver - sa - i   lun gi lan -guen - do   da_ tuoi bei_

ra_____ i   ogn' al-tr og - get-to   è a me fu - nes to   tutto im per -fet - to   tut-to de - tes - to

11) m. 137. E♭ in the earlier editions. Corrected to C minor in this edition.

12) m. 180. Suggested fingerings

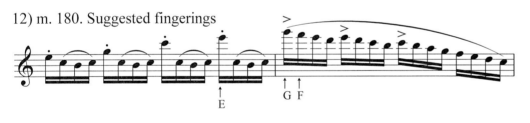

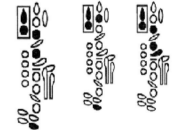

13) m. 204–205. Suggested fingerings

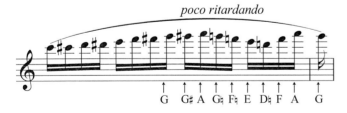

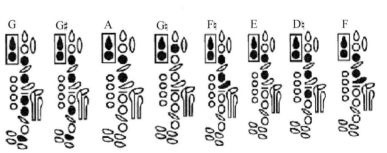

Play the high A and subsequent G, F, E, D, G without the right hand little finger A♭/G♯ key. Add the right little finger G♭/F♯ key for the next A and leave it on for the final G.

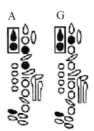

INTRODUCTION, THEME
and VARIATIONS
for Clarinet in B♭ and Piano

Edited with a Newly Arranged
Piano Part by Charles Neidich

GIOACCHINO ROSSINI
(1792–1868)

Introduction (Adagio)

Clarinet in B♭

6

Variation 1

Più mosso

Variation 2

sempre cresc.

Variation 5
Maggiore (Allegro molto)

Clarinet in B♭

* Two cadenzas are provided on pp. 11 and 12.

12

Variation 3

Variation 5
Maggiore (Allegro molto)

Cadenza No. 1
(m. 207)

CHARLES NEIDICH

Cadenza No. 2
(mm. 207)

CHARLES NEIDICH

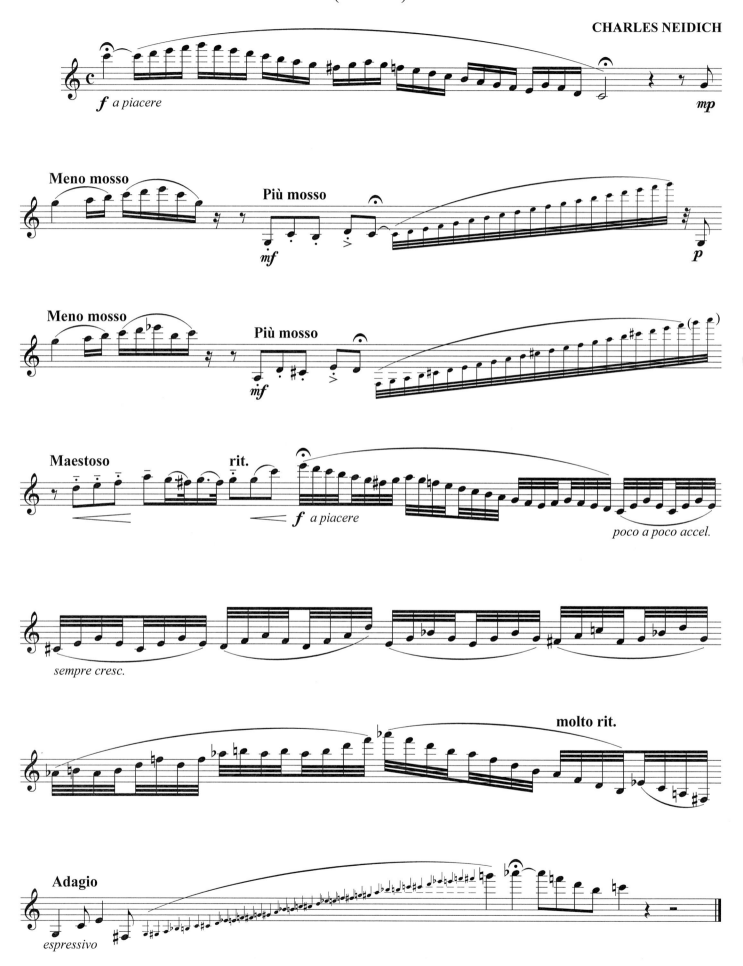

Charles Neidich
21st Century Series for Clarinet

Charles Neidich, hailed by the New Yorker as "a master of his instrument and beyond a clarinetist", has been described as one of the most mesmerizing musicians performing today. Mr. Neidich is on the faculties of the Juilliard School, Queens College of the City University of New York, the Manhattan School, and the Mannes College of Music, and has held visiting positions at the Sibelius Academy in Finland, the Yale School of Music, and Michigan State University. He regularly appears as soloist and as collaborator in programs with major orchestras and chamber ensembles across Europe, Asia, and the United States. Neidich is in demand for master classes throughout the world and known for innovative lecture concerts he has devised. Known both as a leading exponent of period instrument performance practice and as an ardent advocate of new music, Charles Neidich's recordings are available on the Sony Classical, Sony Vivarte, Deutsche Grammophon, Musicmasters, Hyperion, and Bridge labels.

WEBER CONCERTINO FOR CLARINET

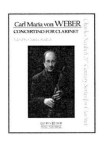

Written for virtuoso clarinetist Heinrich Baermann, Concertino would become the first work of an impressive oeuvre for clarinet, one which along with that of Mozart, Spohr, and Brahms constitutes the backbone of the repertoire. Internationally-recognized clarinetist Charles Neidich unites for the first time Weber's original text with the edition published by Baermann's son, which had formed the basis of most subsequent editions. Also presented are examples from Cyrille Rose's 1879 edition which was the foundation of the French tradition and which held much more closely to Weber's original. This new critical edition inspires those learning the piece to develop their own personal, yet informed interpretation of Weber's premiere clarinet masterpiece. **HL00111948**..$10.95

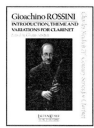

ROSSINI INTRODUCTION, THEME AND VARIATIONS FOR CLARINET

The work is based on two of Rossini's most moving dramatic arias and remains one of the most popular virtuosic works for clarinet to this day. This critical edition by celebrated clarinetist Charles Neidich takes a fresh approach to this work, blending the 19th Century bel canto traditions with a master's perspective on modern clarinet technique. Detailed annotations and historical background equip the clarinetist with an in-depth musical and technical facility to authentically convey the characteristic elegance and drama of Rossini's style. **HL00111949**..$10.95

CAVALLINI 30 CAPRICES FOR CLARINET WITH 2 CD'S

Cavallini was called the 'Paganini of the Clarinet' and was a respected friend and colleague of the most important Italian composers of his day. His 30 Caprices were written to be not merely technical exercises, but studies in style and phrasing. In addition to correcting mistakes and modernizing notation, the noteworthy feature of this edition is clarinetist Charles Neidich's superb recording which is the only complete recording of this classic work. **HL00042367**..$22.95

JEANJEAN 18 ADVANCED ETUDES FOR CLARINET WITH 2 CD'S

Jeanjean, a great virtuoso and prolific writer for the clarinet, attempted in his 18 etudes to write pieces which in addition to being very beneficial to one's technique, would be serious works of music fit for the concert stage. Editor Charles Neidich, hailed by the New Yorker as "a master of his instrument and beyond a clarinetist", brings Jeanjean's Etudes into fresh perspective in this new performance edition. Along with modern, corrected notation and fingerings, the only complete recording is included to demonstrate a characteristic interpretation of the Etudes and to inspire students to explore creative possibilities informed by tradition in their own performances. **HL00042385**............................$20.95

Products and Ordering
www.halleonard.com

Questions or comments?
info@laurenkeisermusic.com